# THE SUPERNATURAL POWER of FORGIVENESS

## KEN. K. OPARAKU

# COPYRIGHT

Unless otherwise indicated, all scripture quotations are taken from the King James Version of the Bible.

# ACKNOWLEDGMENTS

My thanks go to the supernatural and unquestionable God, who gave me this **"DREAM"** decades of years ago when I was still in secondary school and through the Holy Spirit, inspired the writing of this book. To him be all the glory and honour.

Worthy of mention is my spiritual father and mentor Pastor (Dr) and Pastor (Mrs) James Akanbi *(G.O, God's Mercy Revival Ministries, Lagos)*. I also must appreciate Pastor Dallas L. Elder, *(founder/President of Grace Covenant, USA)*, who carefully proof read and foreworded this book, inspite of his crowded schedules.

Also Missionaries Rob & Lori Mangus (U.S.A), not forgetting Pastor and Pastor (Mrs) Benjamin Arazu (U.S.A), Pastor Ebere Nwabuko, Pastor Uche Mbu and Pastor Oliver Egbo, and all the Pastor in Grace Covenant Int'l Nigeria,

To all Pastors, Deacons, Deaconesses, and members of "Heaven Mindset Christian Centre" (HMCC), Lagos, Nigeria.

I must also thank Mrs. Ayo, Bro. Gbenga Adesola of Tentacle magazine, for typing this work.

My appreciation also goes to Mr. Innocent Chukwu, *the Editor-in-Chief, Tentacle Magazine, Lagos* who painstakingly edited and proof read this work.

This acknowledgment will not be complete without the mention of the followings that impacted my life spiritually, Rev. Dr. O. Ezekiel, *(G.O. Christian Pentecostal Mission)*, Rev. Dr. Mercy Ezekiel *(NIC, Christian Pentecostal Mission)*, Rev. & Evang. (Mrs) Chris Kawedo, *(the Delta State co-ordinator, C.P.M. Int'l Asaba)*.

Rev. & Evang. (Mrs.) Godwin. C. Daniel, the Enugu State Coordinator, C.P.M Int'l Owerri, Sir, you really added value to my life.  Also not forgetting Rev. (Mrs) Ego Daniels, *(the Abia State co-ordinator, C.P.M Int'l, Aba)*.

Bro. & Sis. Desmond Okorie; Bro. & Sis. Kanayo Onuoha, Rev. George Azuoma, Elder & Sis. Tony Iwuoma, Pastor & Mrs. David Ifangha, Elder & Sis. Godwin Ani, Evg. Dan Chieke, Rev. Dr. Nnamdi Uba, Mr. Kenneth Uche & Mrs Patience Daniels, Dcns. Edith Lucy Ngozi Allagoa, Mrs Augustina Obiageri Fajuyi, Mrs Dorothy Ihunwo, Pastor Chris Obigwe, Mr & Mrs Samuel Onuawuchi Benson, Elder & Sister Festus Amede, Grace Oparaku, Mr Godwin Oparaku, Mrs Victoria Olachi Lawrence, Roseline Oparaku, Chief & Lolo Tony Benson, Mr. Peter Emeka Benson, Mr. & Mrs. Chibuzor Oparaku, Mr. & Mrs. Samuel Ugochukwu Oparaku, Mrs. Stella Chizor Victor, Mr. Bernard Onyewuchi Nnadi,  Emma Benson, Elder  & Barr. (Mrs) Joeffrey Anah, Pastor & Mrs. Godwin Ogbonna *(RCCG, Lagos)*, Bro. & Sis. Amaechi Basil, you thought I have forgotten you? Not so, for people like you are not easily forgotten.

*Thanks and God bless*

# DEDICATION

This book is dedicated to:

My beloved wife, Juliet Anayo Allagoa Oparaku, who has been my faithful companion, friend, lover and encouragement through all it takes to be the man God wants me to be.

To my lovely children, Noble, Treasure and Virtue who have been down on their knees interceding for me.

# FOREWARD

Ken Oparaku's book, 'The Supernatural Power of Forgiveness' is a rich read. He takes on a very useful topic, forgiveness, an area where people need to know the steps for healing and freedom.

He does an excellent job of weaving scriptural truths, wise counsel and deep ministry experience into this very practical and powerful book.

It is full of quotable quotes and insights that will definitely help people to get beyond the bondage of offences and bitterness in order to live victorious and meaningful lives.

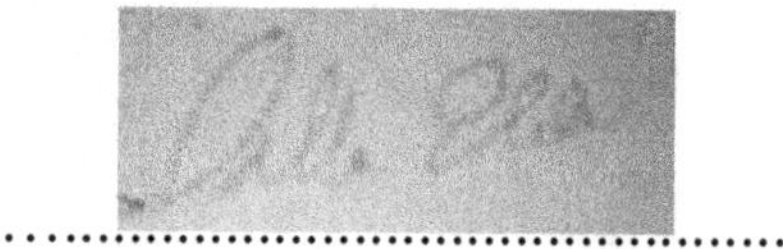

..................................................

***Dallas Los Elder***
*The Apostle and Ministry Director,*
*Grace Covenant International,*
*USA*

# CONTENTS

# INTRODUCTION

If you have once wondered, like me, why some individuals, groups, or even countries all over the world are locked up in the prison house of unforgiveness, then this book is timely.  In fact, my candid observation is that many, both believers and unbelievers have, wittingly or unwittingly, become captives to unforgiveness as they habour grudges, malice, and bitterness in their hearts. Hence, this is why many Christians, Holy Ghost-filled and tongue-talking are still finding it difficult to forgive, particularly preachers who after preaching others into heaven and after performing miracles, may end up in HELL for failing  to forgive others who offended    them.    This    timely    book    on **FORGIVENESS** is for you.

As you carefully read through this book, you will discover why there must be offence, that is, the inevitability and also the necessity of offence.

You will also find out how unforgiveness keeps a Christian    in    bondage    and    in    emotional imprisonment, the medical, spiritual, physical and social implications of holding fellow humans in unforgiveness, the avoidable effects of temperament not touched by the Holy Spirit as well as how to overcome unforgiveness and experience a blissful life which only a forgiving spirit can provide.

Your questions of whom do I forgive and how

many times I am required to tolerate my offenders before I retaliate, are all found in this book.

Another important thing you will find in this book is how you can forgive through unconditional love for fellow humans, that is AGAPE, God's pattern of love that bears no grudge and keeps no record of offences.

Finally, you will discover in this book, the wonders of forgiveness and also the grace made available for forgiveness, to enable you live as a child of God without malice.

I pray that the Holy Spirit of the living God will impart into you **THE SUPERNATURAL POWER OF FORGIVENESS.**

May his grace, henceforth, be made available and sufficient enough for you to forgive those who have offended; hurt, mistreated, blackmailed, castigated, backbitten, raped, cheated and taken advantage of you.

**Ken . K. Oparaku.**

# CHAPTER ONE

# OFFENCE MUST COME

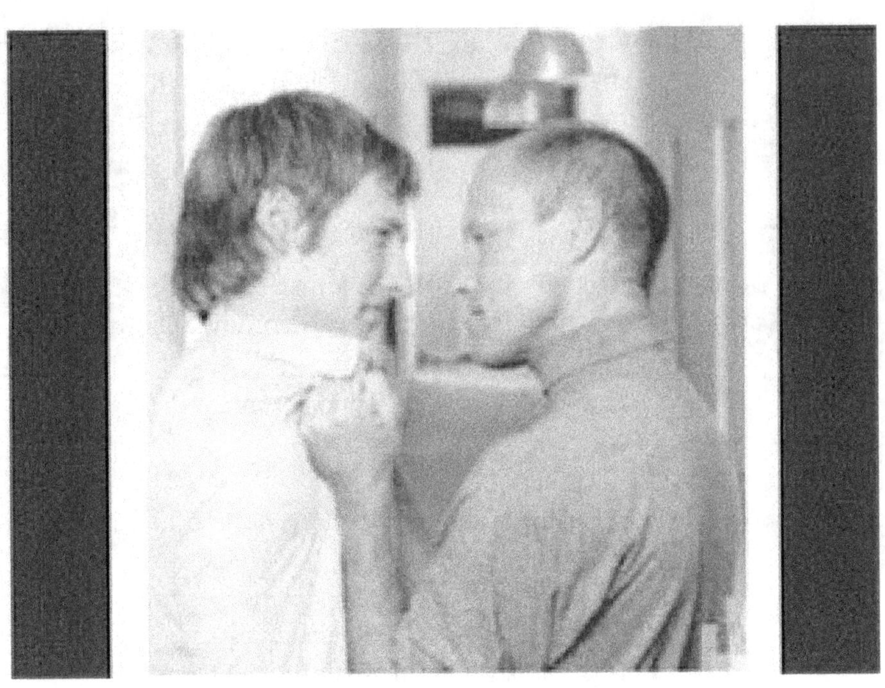

*"Then said he unto the disciples, it is impossible but that offences will come; but woe unto him, through whom they come". Luke 17:1*

We are living in a world of self preservation-the so-called first law of nature where stepping on people's toes and people stepping on your toes, hurting and being hurt, provocation, betrayal, blackmailing one another, cheating on one another and other serious and heart-breaking offences are often expected.

No matter how one tries to stay on his own, he cannot easily run away from this simple truth.

Jesus knew this too well when he decided to arm believers ahead of time with a shield that will help them to remain overcomers at all times.
**tribulation; but be of good cheer; I have overcome the world"**

Jesus also told us that offence must come, but the angles from which this offence will come he did not tell us.
Offence is inevitable and it cannot be prayed off or over spiritualized.

He also told his followers how impossible it is to wish away offences in this scripture:

> **"Then said he unto the disciples,**
> **it is impossible but that offences**
> **will come..."**[2]

The maker of the whole universe had, therefore, told us about the inevitability of the offences in the world.

He is telling us invariably that parents will offend their children and children will offend their parents, husbands, will offend their wives and wives will offend their husbands, teachers will offend their students and vice-versa, business partners will offend one another, employees will offend employers and employers will offend employees,

Brothers will offend sisters and sisters also will offend brothers, bosses will offend subordinates and subordinates will offend their bosses, neighbours will offend one another.

Pastors will offend members and members will offend pastors, senior pastors will offend assistant pastors, assistant pastors will offend the senior pastors.

Since offences cannot easily be avoided, what then are we expected to do whenever they come our way? The answer is simple: we must learn how to forgive and make it flow freely from within us naturally.

Alexander Pope said
**"To err is human, to forgive
is divine".**

## WHAT IS OFFENCE?

Offence occurs when someone is being lightly or deeply

hurt or wounded by the negative actions, statements, remarks or words of another.

When one is offended by another's negative actions, statements, remarks or words, he is bound to be angry. If there is anything people need to guide against, it is offenders who cause them to be angry.

John Hagee once said, **"He who angers you conquers you".**

Offence originated from Satan and he is the cause of offences. Devil may have thought that by offending God, the supreme being would have compromised his divine attributes and outrageously reacted, but to devil's greatest surprise, God placed him where he belonged. For the scripture said in Ezekiel 28:15

*"From the day of your creation you were sheer perfection ... and then imperfection evil, offence, guilt, violence, iniquity was detected in you"* *(emphasis mine)*

No sooner was he cast down from heaven than he started to forment and brew offences on earth, causing man to offend God and his fellow human being. This is because the fallen devil gets fulfilled when man offends God for he thinks that God will throw man out of His presence. But to satan's utter surprise, God had already made provision for the forgiveness of man's sin (offences), before the foundation of the world.

Exposing devil's duplicity, the Bible says,

> *"The serpent was the shrewdest of*
> *all the wild animals the Lord God had*
> *made.  One day he asked the woman;*
> *'Did God really say you must not eat*
> *the fruit from any of the trees in the garden?.*
> *Of course we may eat fruit from the trees in*
> *the garden', the woman replied;*
> *It's only the fruit from the tree in the*
> *middle of the garden that we are not*
> *allowed to eat.  God said,*
> *'You must not eat it or even touch it,*
> *if you do, you will die'.*
> *'You won't die!'*
> *the serpent replied to*
> *the woman...."*[3]
> *(New Living Translation).*

Through deception, Satan made man to doubt and disobey God, thereby ending up in offending God. But God in his infinite mercy and love made provision for the forgiveness of man's disobedience and offence.

> *"And the LORD God made clothing*
> *from animal skins for Adam and his wife"*[4]
> *(New Living Translation).*

Provision for the forgiveness of man's sin (offence) had been put in place before the foundation of the world.

That is, before the sin was actually committed, God had forgiven in advance.

> *:... of the Lamb slain from*
> *the foundation of the world"[5]*

Apostle Paul also has insight into this mystery, thus he said;

> **"According as he hath chosen us**
> **in him before the foundation of the world,**
> **That we should be holy**
> **and without blame before him in love"[6]**

No matter the degree of the offence or provocation, God expects us to forgive, even to forgive in advance.

You should not allow the devil to use anybody to spoil your joy. The purpose for which Satan is causing man to offend God and also his fellow man, is to twist and thwart the cordial relationship between man and God and also man and his fellow human beings.

> **"And they heard the voice of the Lord God**
> **walking in the garden in the cool of the**
> **day: and Adam and his wife hid themselves**
> **from the presence of the LORD GOD**
> **amongst the trees of the garden.**
> **And the LORD GOD called unto Adam,**
> **And said unto him, where art thou?**
> **And he said, I heard thy voice in the**
> **Garden, and I was afraid because**
> **I was naked, and I hid myself"[7]**

Joseph in the book of Genesis. 45:5-8 forgave his

brethren their offences against him, and never counted it against them.  He had even forgiven in advance.

In as much as the Bible said that offence shall come, it did not say you are the one through whom offence will come.

But it said,
*"... but woe unto him, through whom they come"*[8]
Because of this, apostle Paul was very careful not to offend neither God nor man.

> *"And herein do I exercise myself to*
> *have always a conscience void of*
> *offence toward God, and toward men"*[9].

No matter the degree of the offence or provocation, God expects us to forgive or even forgive in Advance.

# CHAPTER TWO

# THE NECESSITY OF FORGIVENESS

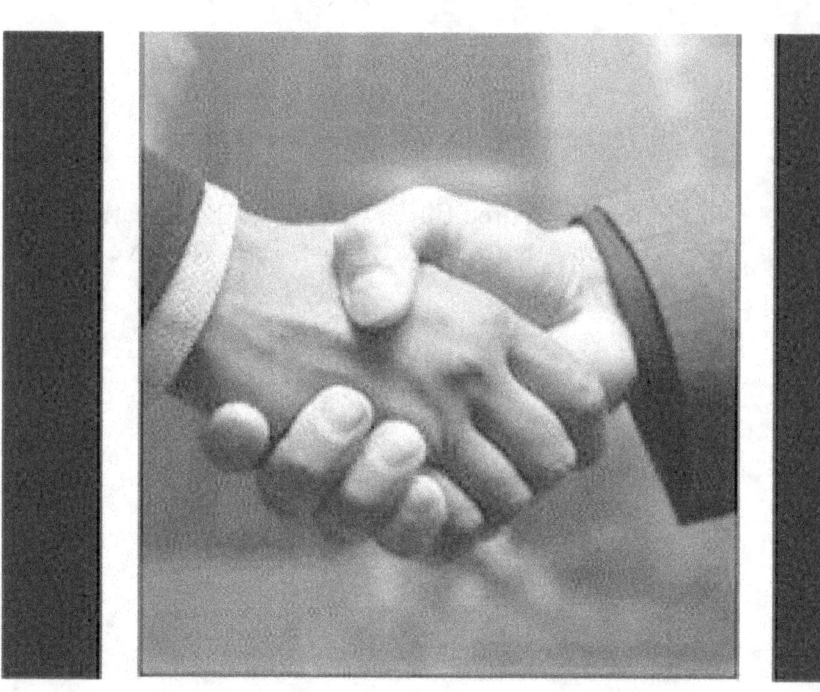

*"Follow peace with all men, and holiness,*
*without which no man shall see the Lord".*
*Heb. 12:14*

God knew before the beginning of the world that man whom he created in his own image and made a free moral agent, would one day offend and sin against him, consequently, he made provision for forgiveness.

*For God so loved the world,*
*That he gave his only begotten son... ..."*[10]

The words **"for"** and **"gave"** joined together to produce the word **"Forgive"** or **"Forgave"**. Thus, because of God's love, he forgave.

There is no book in the world today that talks more about forgiveness than the Bible. The Bible is the only book wherein the doctrine of forgiveness is given prominence.

God emphatically maintained that the only ground on which he would forgive us is when we forgive others.

*"For if ye forgive men their trespasses,*
*your heavenly father will also forgive you;*
*But if ye forgive not men their trespasses,*
*neither will your father forgive your*
*trespasses"*[11]

God is a forgiving father and no matter what we do to offend Him, He forgives us whenever we confess to Him.

So, He has therefore commanded us to forgive others any time they offend us.

No matter the degree of the offence, a Christian who forgives others their offence is always a happy and joyful Christian, while a Christian who does not forgive will always live a life of emotional torture and torment.

Any relationship that lacks forgiveness is heading towards emotional civil war, which may devastate the progress of the people.
Larry James puts it thus:

*"If you are at war with others you cannot be at peace with yourself. You can let go… and forgive! It takes no strength to let go … only courage. Life either expands or contracts in direct proportion to your courage to forgive".*

Forgiveness is not forgetfulness, but some hyper-holiness preachers will tell you to forgive and forget. It is only an imbecile, a moron or one who is suffering from amnesia that can forget anything done to him. In so far as your brain is in good condition and functioning well, you have that mental ability to retain memories of past activities, incidents, pains and hurts.

Even God, who is the originator and source of forgiveness, only forgives but does not forget. Although the Bible says;

*"And their sins and iniquities will I remember no more,"*[12]

the above scriptural reference does not mean that God forgets. God cannot forget because he is 'Omniscient.

Rather, what He does is to separate himself from our confessed and forsaken sins, by deciding not to use them against us anymore.

*"As far as the east is from the west,*
*so far hath he removed our*
*Transgression from us"*[13]

Forgiveness is not condoning evil. That one forgives his offender does not mean that he is condoning or supporting evil. Indeed, forgiveness therefore, should not be viewed as permission, as some are wont to believe, to the offender to continue in his evil ways.

## WHAT IS FORGIVENESS?

"Forgiveness", Mona G. Affinito said, "means deciding not to punish a perceived injustice, taking action on that decision, and experiencing the emotional relief that follows".

Also, Robert Enright sums forgiveness in the following words:
"Forgiveness is giving up the resentment to which you are entitled and offering to the person who hurt you friendlier attitudes to which they are not entitled".

I, therefore, define forgiveness as, "the divine ability to let go the bitterness you feel against those who hurt you either consciously or unconsciously without having the mind to retaliate or intention to

pay back evil with evil anytime you remember it".
God asks us to forgive every one who hurts us no matter the degree or gravity of the hurt.

God is telling you now to forgive that man, that woman, who killed your parents. Forgive that boy or those boys, that man or even your father who sexually assaulted and harassed you. Forgive also that your master who refused to settle you after several years of apprenticeship with him.

Forgive your lecturers who succeeded in making you to have a spill over of one or two years in your four-year degree programme in the university because you refused him sleeping with you.
Also forgive that your father or mother who rejected and abandoned you at infancy, but now that you are grown and have become rich, they are coming back to apologize to you.
Larry James said,

*"Forgiveness breaks the cycle of hatred, resentment, anger and pain that is often passed on to those around you. Forgiveness helps you to make peace with your past."*

Some one said
*"If you want to frustrate your enemies or anyone that hurts you so deeply, give them forgiveness. Forgiveness is the smoothest and sweetest revenge".*
If you understand the psychology, physiology and anatomy of the true nature of forgiveness, and what it really entails, it heals your emotional wounds and makes you healthy spiritually, physically, mentally, socially and materially.

When you forgive you are not doing good to anybody but yourself and yourself alone. Anytime you forgive anyone who offended you, you are practically giving freedom to yourself.

The Holy Spirit made me to know that the word

**"Forgive"** is an acronym, and it means;

**F**reedom from
**O**ver reactions,
**R**esentments,
**G**rudges and
**I**ntravenous
**V**exation of the heart that
**E**ntangles us.

Unforgiveness is self inflicting while forgiveness brings self freedom. Unless you receive freedom from the entanglement of over reaction, resentment, grudges and every other intravenous vexation, you will end up being a prisoner of cadiac arrest and other heart-related sicknesses.
God who is all-knowing, knows fully well that unforgiveness is another name for bondage or imprisonment. Hence he asked us to forgive one another.

It is only a fool or stupid person who will say that he cannot forgive anyone that offends him.

Sometimes ago, God showed me the dangers of

unforgiveness and how destructive it is, by asking me to go and bring a live earth worm, which I did as well. He also told me to bring salt which I did. Could you guess what God wanted to reveal? Of a truth, God is greater than the greatest scientist. He said, "my son, that earth worm represents the heart of man. How fragile and spineless the earth worm is, that is exactly how fragile and delicate the heart is".

And the salt he said represents unforgiveness, resentment, and anger. Now watch out the practical. God said, "now take a pinch of salt and spread it over the earth worm"
No sooner had I spread the salt on the earthworm than it began to twist and disintegrate.

God said, "now, what was your observation?" I said, "the salt was very harmful and destructive to the spineless and fragile earth worm; hence it twisted and disintegrated".

God said, "What you have just seen is exactly what unforgiveness, anger and resentment do to the heart". After my practical with God, I vowed not to habour any unforgiveness, bitterness or malice in my heart because of what that salt did to the earth worm.
No little wonder the Bible said,

*"Keep vigilant watch over your heart; that's where life starts"*[14] *(the message Bible) .*

John Hagee said,

*"Anger is just one letter short of Danger".*

Unforgiveness is self inflicting while forgiveness brings self-freedom. When God is telling you to forgive, it is not for his own good or for the good of someone else, but for your own good. From our practical, I think you see what salt did to that earthworm, that is what unforgiveness, anger, resentment, bitterness and malice do to the heart.

When you forgive, you receive freedom from the entanglement of outrage, over-reaction, resentment, grudge and every other intravenous vexation of the heart that are capable of causing cadiac arrest and other heart-related sicknesses.

*"A happy heart is good medicine and a cheerful mind works healing, but a broken spirit dries up the bones"[15] (Amplified Version)*

*"A cheerful disposition is good for your health; gloom and doom leave you bone-tired"[15] (The message Bible)*

*"A cheerful heart is good medicine, but a broken spirit saps a person's strength"[15] (Life Application New Living Translation)*

The only thing unforgiveness can do in your life is to make your heart and face very gloomy and faint. It finally dries up your bones. But forgiveness gives you freedom from these harmful feelings, and makes you happy, joyful and ultimately healthy.

Friend, having seen what unforgiveness does to the heart, do you still go on asking: "should I still forgive him/her…?" The next chapter provides solution to this poser.

# CHAPTER THREE

## SHOULD I STILL FORGIVE HIM?

*"You are a slave to that man or
that woman you have vowed never to forgive"*

There are offences, deep hurts or pains one may consider terminal, irreconcilable or unpardonable. And these are the offences some people have vowed never to forgive the offender(s).

"Should I still forgive…?" Or how can I forgive?" have been the often asked questions.

Friends, there is no where in the Bible that God permits you to hold any body on the neck and squeeze life out of him because of the deep hurts or pains they caused you.

Your senses can give you one hundred and one reasons why you should not forgive that boy that raped you; those people that killed your parents; that business partner that betrayed you, that brother or that sister that blackmailed you; that half brother/sister that mistreated you; your spouse that cheated on you and on and on.

But God is saying, my son, my daughter, I forgave you, I did not consider the gravity of your offences, therefore you should forgive others.

Considering what King Saul did to David, human senses would have answered "No" to the question, "Should I still forgive…", but David was a different person who had the grace to forgive.

Friend, forgiving and letting go of the deep hurts and pains can be a very difficult challenge, but it is even more difficult, stressful and devastating to hold on to grudges and resentments.

**"The weak can never forgive.
Forgiveness is the attribute
of the strong"**
*- Mahatma Gandhi.*

In spite of all the deep hurts and pains King Saul inflicted on David, he (David) forgave Saul. Friend, have you in your heart truly forgiven those who have inflicted deep hurts, pains and wounds on you?  Know that, no hurt is too hot that it cannot be forgiven.

> *"And the men of David said unto him,*
> *behold the day of which the Lord said unto*
> *thee, behold, I will deliver thine enemy into*
> *thine hand, that thou may do to him as it*
> *shall seem good unto thee.*
> *Then David arose, and cut off the skirt*
> *of Saul's robe privily.  And it came to*
> *Pass afterward, that David's heart smote*
> *Him, because he had cut off Saul's*
> *skirt..."[16]*

In the same manner, Stephen, one of the early apostles who was stoned to death by haters of the gospel, while he endured the painful death, was able to exhibit a life of forgiveness.  He called on God to have mercy and forgive his murderers.  This is because forgiveness is not at all something we have to do, but something we must allow to flow through us.

> *"And they stoned Stephen, calling upon God,*
> *and saying, Lord Jesus, receive my Spirit.*
> *And he kneeled down, and cried with a*
> *loud voice, Lord; Lay not this sin to their*

> ***charge. And when he had said this,***
> ***He fell asleep"*** [17]

Stephen was able to forgive because the grace was made available for him and he also prayed for those that stoned him to death because he loved them; and would let go anything that would poison him within.

Mr. X asked, "Should I still forgive my wife considering the deep hurts, wounds and pains she inflicted on me?"

Now hear this true life story  Mr. X loved his wife Mrs. Z and had been caring and providing for her needs.

But for Mrs. Z, despite all that the husband did to make her happy, became unfaithful to him and was having extra-marital affairs with other men.  In the process, she had four male children whom Mr. X loved so much with passion but never knew that he was not the biological father of those four children.

They were all grown ups and the youngest among the four was about fourteen years old when Mrs. Z repented and gave her life to Christ, bubbling in the Lord with zeal.

Not long afterward, having basked in the euphoria of her tender faith, her conscience began to condemn her and as the feeling of guilt could not allow her to rest until she decided to go and make confession.

Having prayed, she went straight to her husband

and narrated the whole story, how she had those four children outside marriage.  Hell was let loose and Mr. X couldn't believe his ears.  To him, it was like he was dreaming.

His heart ran into his stomach and he became confused, not knowing what to do.  Is it to kill his wife, the children and himself?

He looked at the four children he used to be fond of, and they were also fond of him, how another man would come and claim them because his Deoxyribonucleic Acid (DNA) was not in them.
If you were mr. X what will you do?

**God said, "...Forgive and you will be forgiven"[18]**

Let's hear the voice of Larry James;

**"Forgiveness is the most single process that brings peace to our soul and harmony to our life.  All of us at some point in our lives, have been hurt and wounded by actions or words of another. Sometimes the grievances have been so great we thought, no way, this I cannot forgive"**

Resentment and hostility can run so deep that forgiveness becomes very difficult.  We feel we have a right to our indignation.
Friend, were you abused as a child; has your trusted friend betrayed you?  Did your mother abandon you at a tender age and fled? Did your father reject and disown you?
Did your brothers and sisters dispossess you of your

father's inheritance? Did you raise up your hand from the pit of life's difficulties, yet nobody around cared to give you a helping hand? Were you molested sexually?

God is beckoning on you and asking you to forgive. You forgive not for the sake of the person that offended you, but for your own sake.

Beloved, know this truth, you will never be free until you learn how to forgive others.

***You are a slave to that man or that woman you have vowed never to forgive.***

Refusing to forgive those that hurt you implies choosing to remain in torture, torment and prison of unforgiveness.

And this has caused terrible sicknesses to so many people, and has destroyed the health of so many people and sent some to untimely grave.
My friend, why don't you deliver yourself from this great and terrible sickness that can cause untimely death by simply forgiving those that have offended you?

# CHAPTER FOUR

# UNFORGIVENESS IS IMPRISONMENT

*"Unforgiveness, bitterness or resentment is an emotional prison that hinders one from receiving God's unspeakable blessings". Ken. K. Oparaku*

The truth of the matter is that unforgiveness puts one in a great bondage. It builds high walls of prison and imprisons anyone who holds on to it and keeps grudges, malice, hostility and bitterness in his heart. It is these high walls of imprisonment that hinder God from showering his unspeakable blessings upon your life. These prison walls of unforgiveness can also hinder your prayers from being answered.

It also stops men from coming closer to you. It stops the favour of God from coming within your reach. It stops you from fulfilling your God's given dreams. It keeps you from enjoying good health and harmony in your marriage.

Forgive everyone who hurts you no matter the gravity of the offence so that you can get out of the prison of unforgiveness. Many a times we mistakenly think that we forgive others for their sake. But this is not true, when we forgive; we are not doing it for other person's good but for our own good.

*"And the Lord turned the captivity (imprisonment) of Job, when he prayed for his friends (Forgave his friends): also the Lord gave Job twice as much as he had before (double restoration).*

*Then came there unto him all his brethren,*
*and all his sisters,*
*and all they that had been of his acquaintance*
*before and eat bread with him in his house*
*(reunion ship)*

*And they...."19*

*"When Job prayed for his friends, the*
*Lord restored his fortunes.  In fact, the*
*Lord gave him twice as much as before!*

*Then all his brothers, sisters, and former*
*friends came and feasted with him in his*
*home.  And they consoled him and*
*comforted him..."20* (Life application
New Living Translation)

*"After Job had interceded for his friends,*
*God restored his fortune  and then*
*doubled it!  All his brothers and sisters*
*and friends came to his house and*
*celebrated..."21* (The Message Bible)

Job experienced a turn around from captivity when he prayed for his friends; this implied that Job forgave his friends.

Also, he experienced double-fold restoration of all that he lost, and finally, Job enjoyed a reunion fellowship, peace of mind and there was harmony between him and his friends and other relations of his.

Do you want peace of mind, reunionship, harmony, understanding and love between you and your friends and other relations?  Then forgive them their faults.

*"Resentment is an emotional prison built brick by brick, hurt by hurt, and tear by tear"* John Hagee

Friend, you've been in that prison house of unforgiveness for too long, it is high time you came out of it through forgiveness so that you will enjoy your freedom.

The fact is this, you are a slave to the person you have not forgiven. If you want to remain a slave to that man, woman, boy or girl, then keep holding them to unforgiveness, bitterness and grudge. But if you do not want to remain a slave to people, learn how to forgive everyday.

You may say, "Ken, but it is hard to do", yes, the Bible did not say all things are simple or easy, but Bible said:
**"...All things are possible"**[22]

According to Paul Tillich, "genuine forgiveness is participation, reunion, overcoming the powers of estrangement..."

You can decide today to come out from the aforementioned prison by forgiving everyone so as to be free from the implications of unforgiveness.

*"When you hold resentment toward another you are bound to that person by an emotional link that is stronger than steel. Forgiveness is the only way To dissolve that link and get free"*,
**Says Catherine Ponder.**

# CHAPTER FIVE

# THE IMPLICATIONS OF UNFORGIVENESS

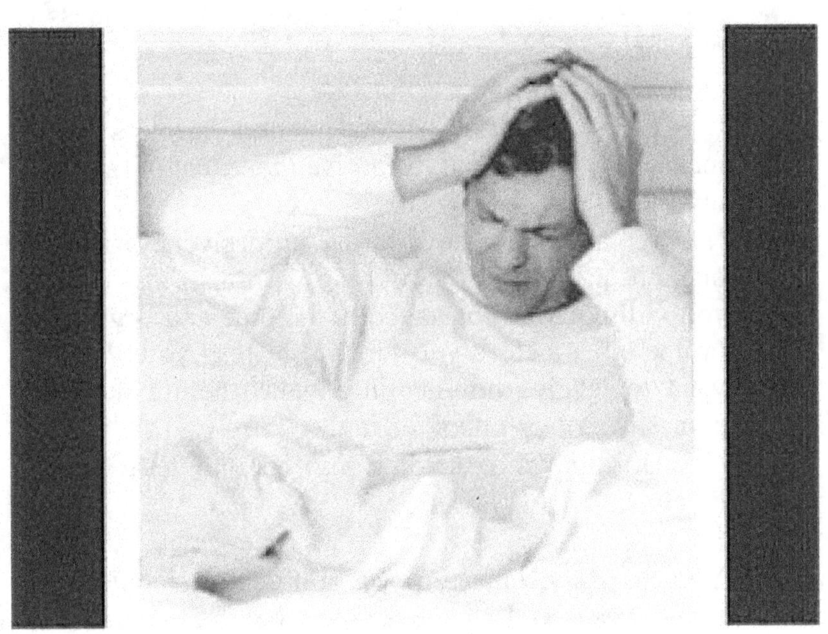

***"Nothing on earth devastates one's health, one's relationship with man and God, more than unforgiveness". Ken. K. Oparaku***

Unforgiveness, as devastating, destructive and cancerous as it is, does not even scare people, but they always romance with it.

Spouse vowed not to forgive her partner, brother vowed not to forgive his brother, sister vowed not to forgive her sister, friend vowed not to forgive his friend, neighbour vowed not to forgive his neighbour, children vowed not to forgive their parents, pastor vowed not to forgive his members, and members vowed not to forgive their Pastor, business partner vowed not to forgive his business partner.

It is gross ignorance or total mental darkness that makes one to vow not to forgive those that offended him/her.

If you know how devastating unforgiveness is to one's health, one's relationship with man and God, you will not wait for anybody to come and beg you or apologise before you forgive, instead you would want to forgive him/her in advance before he/she comes begging or apologizing.

No matter how hot that hurt may be, only let go and let come.

You may say, but Ken you don't understand! My friend, yes I do. I have been there before, therefore I know how you are feeling.

I was blackmailed, told lies against and treated badly by those that were once blessed through the grace of God upon my life but I gave them forgiveness for my own sake and heaven's sake.

Is there anyone you are keeping anger, resentment, bitterness and grudge against in your heart? Forgive, so that the great burden of unforgiveness will not weigh you down spiritually, physically, mentally and socially.

What unforgiveness does to any man that keeps it in his heart is what the ancient Persians did to any man found guilty of murder.

When the ancient Persians found a man guilty of murder, they punished him by strapping the corpse of his victim to his back. The weight of the corpse dragged the man down, the presence of it constantly tormented him, and the sight and smell of it scared others away. At last, it robbed him of his life.

Bob Grass said,

***"Nothing is heavier than bitterness".***

By the reason of the above consequences and implications, Apostle Paul came up with this advice;

> ***"Let all bitterness, and wrath, anger
> and clamour, evil speaking, be put away
> from you, with all malice. And be ye kind
> one to another, tender-hearted, forgiving
> one another, even as God for Christ's sake
> hath forgiven you"*** [23]

Bible scholars, scientists, researchers and academics through their findings, have come to a very logical conclusion that the consequences of unforgiveness medically, physically, mentally, spiritually and otherwise are very colossal. These are some of the implications:

## MEDICAL IMPLICATIONS

## I.  IT ATTACKS THE IMMUNE SYSTEM:-

If you    understand the psychology, physiology and anatomy of unforgiveness, how destructive and killing it is, you will not keep it in your heart anymore. It breaks    down one's immune system, thereby allowing all sorts of sicknesses like malaria, cancer, loss of appetite that can lead to ulcer, to blossom in the body. Unforgiveness is a very good strengthener of other    terminal diseases. It can cause fatigue, heart failure,   high   blood   pressure   and   ultimately paralysis.

But forgiveness heals the body diseases faster through love, joy, happiness, smiles, laughter and rejoicing.

**"A merry heart doeth good like a medicine; but a   broken spirit dries the bones"**[24]

Hence the advice of Apostle Paul to Christians, "…

**"…Rejoice evermore"**[25]

## ii.  IT       RELEASES       ADRENALINE:-

Unforgiveness   and   keeping   of   anger,   malice, grudge, and            resentment   cause   the discharge of adrenaline in the   body system and this affects negatively, blood circulation,   energy,   pulse, respiration   and   digestion.   It   encourages   stress   and depression.

Beloved, if actually you want to enjoy an improved circulatory, respiratory and digestive system, you have to do away with unforgiveness and try as much as possible to forgive one another.

> *"...lest any root of bitterness springing up trouble you. And thereby many be defiled"*[26]

### iii.  IT CAUSES CARDIAC ARREST:-

Unforgiveness has been linked with heart problem, stroke, chronic pains, eye problem, loss of memory, and Parkinson syndrome, and above all, it shortens one's life
span.

> *"...but it came to pass in the morning,*
> *when the wine was gone out of Nabal,*
> *and his wife had told him these*
> *things, that his heart died within him,*
> *and he became as a stone.*
> *And it came to pass about ten days*
> *after, that the Lord smote*
> *Nabal that he died"*[27]

Nabal was the first victim of Cardiac arrest, stroke and paralysis from creation.

## 2.    SPIRITUAL IMPLICATIONS

### i.  UNANSWERED PRAYERS: (Mark 11:25)

Unforgiveness, as deadly and destructive as it is, does not scare christians, but many choose to accommodate it.
Does it cause you to wonder why your prayer has

not been answered?  Look around and see if there is anybody you are keeping bitterness and grudges against in your heart, then forgive them so that your prayers may be answered.

**"And when you stand praying forgive…"**[28]

## ii.   IT CAN SEND ONE TO HELL:-

We have heard      testimonies  by  those  who died and were privileged to   come   back   to   life about, how some dedicated, faithful  and committed christians went to hell       because        of unforgiveness. If that is the case, friend, you have to take   your   time   how   you   accommodate unforgiveness in your heart, lest it drags you to hell.

According  to  Rev.  Dr.  O.  Ezekiel  the  General Overseer of Christian Pentecostal Mission Int'l he said *"I have learnt to forgive in advance"*.

This  is  exactly  what  any  other  Christian  should learn to do.  Why don't you repent from the sin of unforgiveness and ask God for the grace to forgive? How would you feel if at last you found yourself in hell  and  were  told  that  what  put  you  there  was because  you  refused  to  forgive  that  man,  woman, boy, girl?
Be wiser today, learn to forgive every day lest you end up in hell.

*"And his Lord was wrath, and delivered*
*him to the tormentors, till he should*
*pay all that was due unto him.  So likewise*
*shall my heavenly father do also unto you,*

*if you from your hearts forgive not*
*everyone his brother their trespasses"*[29]

**iii. IT CONTAMINATES OUR PERSONALITIES:-** Christians who keep grudges, malice, resentment and bitterness due to unforgiveness, do not realize that they are doing so to the detriment of their lives. Unforgiveness is a toxic waste, which is capable of poisoning its victim (that accommodates it). When you don't forgive, you are not hurting anybody but yourself because the person you're keeping it against may not know. If you want to live a joyful and happy Christian life, be quick to forgive and also according to Rev. Dr. O. Ezekiel, learn how to forgive in advance. To enjoy a healthy Christian life, avoid bitterness in the heart.

*"That no one cultures a root of*
*bitterness to cause a disturbance*
*by which the majority shall be*
*contaminated" Berk. Eph 4:31-32*

A Christian who finds it difficult to forgive others has bitterness rooted in his heart and the fruits this root of bitterness bears will not be healthy for the person and for others also, because it does contaminate one's personality and relationship.

## 3. SOCIAL IMPLICATION.

Being unable to forgive by holding on to bitterness, malice, grudges, resentment can make a relationship, organization, institution, company, school or church    miserable, ineffective and unproductive.This is because a vindictive mind-set is very cancerous and can spread its bitterness all over the environment, which might likely contaminate others. Nothing moves forward in an environment of unforgiveness.

According to Guy Finley,
*"...so, if we won't let go of  some  pain,  whose time has now past, then who is to blame for the weight of this burden still being carried on our back?"*

If not for the intervention of God in the life of King David,  the  malice,  grudges,  resentment  and bitterness Ahithophel kept in his heart against King David,  would  have  wrecked  his  kingdom. Ahithophel was a choice and cherised friend of King  David.  He was a native of Giloh, a town in the hill country of Judah.  He was King David's personal  Adviser (P.A).  He knew the word of God and had the understanding and wisdom that only come from the application of the word of God. According to 2 Samuel 16:23, "his advice was as if one inquired of the word of God".  Of a truth, he was a walking encyclopedia of the word, King David and his son Absalom trusted his advice.  But David never knew that he was keeping resentment and bitterness against him for many good years because he killed his son-in-law, Uriah

Due to gross unforgiveness, Ahithophel conspired with Absalom against David.  Ahithophel had a son by name Eliam, Eliam had a daughter named Bathsheba.   Ahithopel  was  the  grandfather  of

Bathsheba whom King David seduced and slept with. Consequently she became pregnant and this led to the  murder of Uriah by David; Ahithophel's son-in-law, and a valiant soldier in King David's army. This was the reason why he gave Absalom that counsel on how he could kill David and his men. Due to unforgiveness he betrayed his true friend, David, but God  was with David and Absalom did not follow the counsel of Ahithopel, for if he had followed that counsel, David and his men would have been killed. God turned Ahithophel's counsel to foolishness in the ears of Absalom through the counsel of Hushai. Hence, Ahithophel committed suicide because his counsel was disregarded (2 Sam. 17).

# CHAPTER SIX

# YOUR TEMPERAMENT AND FORGIVENESS

*"...Your honest faith- and what a rich faith it is,
handed down from your grand-mother
Lois to your mother Eunice, and now to you!"*
*II Timothy 1:4-5*

**P**eople behave the way they do and do the things they do as a result of traits which are conveyed by the genes through the vehicle of hereditary.

The above is the major reason why children do resemble their father, mother or any other person in the family lineage.

The way you act and react, behave or do things is determined by the temperamental factors that recycle in your family lineage.

> *It was no little wonder Levi out of anger and unforgiveness killed Shechem and all the males in the city for raping his sister, Dinah.*[30]

Moses, also the grandson of Levi, out of anger and unforgiveness killed an Egyptian. Can you see how anger and unforgiveness recycled in the family lineage of Levi? Parents, what are you passing on to your children? Good or bad traits?

If you are a liar, a thief, adulterer, fraud or a trickstar, definitely you will give birth to children who will emulate what they see you do.
The children and grand children of Abraham copied lying from him.

So also did the children and grandchildren of David copy immoral life from their father David.
Parents should be extremely careful about how they live their lives, for it can affect their children

negatively.  For we will definitely give account of our lives to God.

**WHAT IS TEMPERAMENT? "Temperament is the combination of inborn traits that subconsciously affect all our behaviour"** Tim Lahaye.

I therefore define temperament as "a combination of inherent traits from one's parents which reveals areas of natural weakness and natural strength, that makes one to behave the way he/she does". This is the common reason why a child behaves either like the father or the mother. These inherent traits are the combination of the tendencies of our fathers and mothers.

*"Then answered Jesus and said unto them, verily, verily,*
*I say unto you, the son can do nothing of himself, but what he seeth the father do, for what things soever he doeth, these also doeth the son likewise"*
*John 5:19* [31]

Also apostle Paul confirmed these inherent traits in Timothy
**"...Your honest faith- and what a rich faith it is, handed down from your grand-mother Lois to your mother Eunice, and now to you!"**
**II Timothy 1:4-5**

**Phlegmatic** may look calm and quiet on the outside, but they are prone to anger and resentment. They can habour malice, grudges and resentment for a very long time and above all, they find it difficult to forgive. They are very vengeful.

Simeon and Levi are examples of phlegmatic.
*Simeon and Levi are brethren; instruments of cruelty are in their habitations o my soul, come not thou into their secret; unto their assembly, mine honour, be not thou united; for in their anger they slew a man and in their self-will they digged down a wall"[32]*
**Choleric** are very hot-tempered, violent and can explode in anger at anytime. They also bear grudges; they are very vengeful and can go to any extent to repay evil for evil. Paul is an example of choleric.

*"Alexander the coppersmith did me much evil; the Lord reward him according to his works.."[33]*

**Sanguine** can easily be angered, but one good thing about them is that they easily apologize if they are at fault or easily forgive if they are offended. Simon Peter is a good example of Sanguine.

*"Then Simeon Peter having a sword drew it, and smote the high priest's servant, and cut off his right ear. The servant's name was Malchus"[34]*

Melancholies like phlegmatic are introverted. They are perfectionist and good analysts, and very orderly. He responds to variety of moods. When he is better off, he is triggered into the height of ecstasy and when he is worse off, he withdraws into his shell. He looks sad, gloomy and depressed. He keeps records of the evil done to him. Moses is an example of melancholy.

But, when these temperaments are touched by and come under the control of the Holy Spirit, forgiving one another will no more be a problem to them. Then forgiveness flows naturally from within their hearts because the Holy Spirit has taught them how to overcome unforgiveness.

Friend, it does not matter the temperamental factors that have been recycling in your family lineage. Now that you have given your life to Jesus Christ and accepted him as your personal Lord and Saviour, you have obtained a new deoxyribonucleic acid (DNA) called Divine Nature Ability (DNA), tracing you to the family lineage of our Lord Jesus Christ.

The traits, genes, and chromosomes you inherited from your family lineage will no more influence you because you now have the divine genes, traits and chromosomes of your heavenly Father. Thereby enabling you to act and behave like your heavenly Father and no more like your earthly father.

*"Beloved, now are we the sons of God, and itdoth not yet appear what we shall be; but we know that when he shall appear, we shall all be like him; for we shall see him as he is"35A (KJV) "But friends, that's exactly who we are; children of God; and that's only the beginning. Who knows how we'll end up! What we know is that when Christ is openly revealed, we'll see him and in seeing him, become like him" 35B (The Message Bible).*

***"Whereby are given unto us
exceeding, great and precious
promises; that by these ye might
be partakers of the divine nature"[36]***

At the point of salvation man's spirit is recreated and filled with the divine nature of God which is love and he will then begin to have the tendencies of God in his spirit, through renewing his mind by the word of God. If your mind is not renewed by the word of God, your spirit cannot manifest Christlikeness in your life. But because the father's divine nature is imparted to you, automatically you will come into union with God the Father, and the Son and of the Holy Spirit.

You will no more hate but love, no more keep unforgiveness, malice, resentment, bitterness, and the like, but forgiving all.

***"...Ye are of God my little children"[37]***

Because ye are of God, therefore, you will forgive as God forgives, love as God loves, care as God cares, show kindness as he shows.

Friends, you came from above and as such your family lineage's traits, genes and chromosomes should in no wise influence you any more because, **"He that cometh from above, is above all.'** I see you overcoming what your father and mother, even your fore-fathers, couldn't overcome.

The Holy Spirit of the living God will this day

empower you to overcome all the negative traits and genes that have recycled in your family lineage, in Jesus name.

For anger, wrath, unforgiveness and other negative traits and genes will no more overcome and control you, for you are no more under them but above them.

*"But God, who is rich in mercy, for his great love wherewith he loved us, even when we were dead in sins, hath quickened us together with Christ, (by grace ye are saved) And hath raised us up together, in heavenly Places in Christ Jesus"*[38]

*"Far above all principality, and power, and might,  and dominion, and every name that is named, (anger, wrath, unforgiveness, immoral habits and other weaknesses) not only in this world, but also in that which is to come"*[39]

# HOW TO OVERCOME UNFORGIVENESS

*"Don't keep record of any evil done to you either in your diary, calendar or in your heart".*
*Ken. K. Oparaku*

Unforgiveness is a plague that needs to be combated and overcome before it destroys one's health, finance, spiritual life, relationship, marriage and business.

Unforgiveness can be gotten rid of and replaced with forgiveness through the power of the Holy Spirit.
Without the intervening power of the Holy Spirit, one will remain a slave to unforgiveness.

Below are the steps provided by the Holy Spirit on how to overcome unforgiveness:-

**i. ACKNOWLEDGE IT:-** Don't justify yourself or give one hundred and one reasons why you must not forgive. Unforgiveness is a sin; don't give it a baptismal name or a lighter name. Call it a sin and acknowledge it as sin, then you will receive the grace to overcome it. This step is also applicable to overcoming any other sin.

> *"For I acknowledge my transgressions: and my sin is ever before me"*[40]

**ii. CONFESS IT:-** Make sure that you confess every sin of unforgiveness. Don't allow it to linger in your heart because it will be very disastrous and devastating if you do.

> *"If we confess our sins, He is faithful and just to forgive us our sins and to cleanse us from all unrighteousness"*[41]

## DECISIVE STEPS

To overcome unforgiveness, you have to take a decisive step to free yourself from keeping any resentment, grudge or malice in your heart no matter what happened.  This, you cannot do by your own strength, but must depend on the strength of the Holy Spirit, and the grace of the Almighty God.  The Holy Spirit of the living God has helped so many Christians to overcome unforgiveness and He is waiting also to help you overcome unforgiveness if and only if you can call upon him to help you.

> *"Likewise you also, reckon yourselves*
> *to be dead indeed to sin, but alive to*
> *God in Christ Jesus our Lord.  Therefore*
> *do not let sin reign in your mortal body,*
> *that you should obey it in its lusts.*
> *And do not present your members*
> *as instruments of unrighteousness*
> *to sin, but present yourselves to*
> *God as being alive from dead,*
> *and your members as instruments*
> *of righteousness to God"*[42]

**TAKE *"PRAYERQUINE"* EVERYDAY:-** The enemy *knows* what prayer is and what prayer can do in your life, that is why he tries to weaken your prayer life and keeps you bound in chains and shackles of unforgiveness; thus making it impossible for you to overcome it.

*Prayerquine* attacks, subdues and overcomes all the unforgiving hormones in your body stream. Make sure that you don't go out each day without a full dosage of it.

Unless you recognize and acknowledge the propensity of the unforgiving hormones in your blood streams, you cannot fight against it with the full dosage of *Prayerquine*. Rather, you will always be vulnerable to it.

I challenge you today to kneel down and begin to take your *Prayerquine* dose every day, then ask God to drain the fluid of unforgiveness in your blood stream.

> ***"…Howbeit this kind goeth not out but by prayer and fasting"43***

**SEARCH THE SCRIPTURE:-** Satan, the enemy and tempter tried to get Jesus Christ to submit and bow to his temptations, but each time Jesus fired back with the word of God- ***"It is written…"***

This happened repeatedly, until the third time, Satan disappeared and left Him alone.

This signified that the devil cannot flex muscle with a child of God who knows the word and his authority in Christ and always stands on the word of God.

Your spiritual strength, power, stamina and vitality, is directly proportional to the volume of the word of God you are able to consume, and your victory depends on this.

The word of God is also life.  The Greek translation for **"WORD"** is **"SPERMA"**, meaning life.  God's word is His very life and seed. The word works wonders and it is creative; as you read it and retain it in your heart and not your head, it will make you to overcome any sin and temptation.

*"Search the scriptures; for in them*
*ye think ye have eternal life;*
*and they are they which testify of me"[44]*

Power to overcome sin and temptation comes from the word of God. If you want to overcome the sin of unforgiveness, search and study the scriptures.

*"Great peace have they which love thy law; and*
*nothing shall offend them"[45]*

## INTERCEDE FOR THE PERSON, THE OFFENDER.

If you want to overcome unforgiveness, particularly when the hurt is too deep and you wouldn't naturally as a man Like to forgive, you can forgive by praying for the offender. Job overcame unforgiveness by praying for those that offended him.

*"And the LORD turned the captivity*
*of Job, when he prayed for his friends:*
*also the LORD gave Job twice as*
*much as he had before"[46]*

*Stephen also overcame unforgiveness*
*by praying for those that stoned*
*him to death.[47]*

You too can overcome unforgiveness if you, from

today, begin to intercede for those that terribly hurt you.

## CONSIDER THE OFFENDER AS A CHILD.

No matter how grievous that offence is, you can overcome it by considering those who offended you as children. If you have this mentality, there is no hurt too hot, that you can't forgive.

Have this mentality; I must forgive because the offender is still a child though he/she may be an adult.

*"When I was a child, I spoke as a child..."*[48]

## SHOW LOVE TO THE PERSON:

The foundation of Christianity is nothing but love in our day to day relationship with people. God showed us how to love and how to forgive through love by forgiving us our sins because of love.

*"A new commandment I give*
*unto you, that ye love one another;*
*as I have loved you that ye also love*
*one another. By this shall all men*
*know that ye are my disciples,*
*if ye have love one to another"*[49]

If we are practitioners of love, there is no hurt, resentment, blackmail, offence, rape or injustice that we cannot forgive.

*"And above all things have fervent*
*charity (love) among yourselves for*

*charity shall cover the multitude of sin"*[50]
*(KJV)*

*"Most of all, love, each other as if
your life depended on it, Love makes
up for practically anything"* [51]
*(The Message)*

Let love have perfect work in your life and you will learn how to forgive from your heart any hurt, bitterness or offence.

# THE SCOPE OF FORGIVENESS

*"Our capacity to make peace with another
person and with the world depends very
much on our capacity to make peace with ourselves".*
*N. H. Thich*

Forgiving one another should cut across the border or boundary of your family, village, kindred, community, state or nation.

I used to hear some people say, "why must I reconcile or forgive him? Is he my father/mother, brother/sister, relation or friend?"

This statement originated and came from the pit of hell because God did not at any time ask you to forgive only your family members, neighbours, colleagues, friends or members of your church or organization. But that you should forgive anyone, anywhere, anytime throughout the whole world.

## FORGIVENESS SHOULD NOT BE DISCRIMINATORY

God did not permit us to be discriminatory because he too is not discriminatory in forgiving the world their sins. He did not say that he would only forgive the Jews and raise sledgehammer over the heads of the Gentiles. He forgave the world, both the Jews and the Gentiles, their sins.

> *"Is he the God of the Jews only?*
> *Is he not also of the Gentiles?*
> *Yes, of the Gentiles also"*[52]

Also the Holy Spirit through Apostle Paul encourages us to;

> *"Follow peace with all men and*
> *holiness, without which no man*
> *shall see the Lord"*[55]

When was the last time somebody betrayed,

mistreated and hurt you?  Just take a walk through the corridors of your memory; whom do you see or meet with?  O! That man/woman that offended and mistreated you, whom you vowed never to forgive?  Can you stretch forth your hand and give him Friend, if God does not discriminate, who are you to discriminate and decide those you will forgive and those you will not forgive?

God is telling you to forgive one another's offences and mistakes.
The phrase, "One another" means person of the same family, church, school, company, organization, tribe or culture.

It could also mean "among yourselves".  The Holy Spirit of God, through Apostle Paul, is asking us to forgive ourselves no matter the gravity, heaviness or degree of the offence, because if you do, it goes a very long way to encourage unity in the families, churches, companies schools, organizations and also among husbands and wives

*"Let all bitterness, and wrath, anger and*
*clamour, evil speaking, be put away*
*from you, with all malice.*
*And be ye kind one to another,*
*tender-hearted, forgiving one another,*
*even as God for Christ's sake*
*hath forgiven you"*[53]

God also went beyond this, and told us to forgive men their sins. The word MEN means others or outsiders.  This shows that we should not only forgive those that are of the same family, church, organization, tribe or company with us. The spirit of forgiveness says that, "you should also forgive those outsiders that are not members of your family, church, organization".

> *"For if ye forgive men their trespasses, your heavenly father will also forgive you;  But if ye forgive not men their trespasses, neither will your father forgive your trespasses"[54]*

a very warm handshake and tell him that you love and care for him and that have decided to forgive him?

> *"...And be at peace among yourselves"[56]*

**"Our capacity to make peace with another person and with the world depends very much on our capacity to make peace with ourselves"** *Thich Nhat Hahn.*

**"Let all bitterness and indignation and wrath (passion, rage, bad-temper) and resentment (anger, animosity) and quarrelling (brawling, clamour, contention) and slander (evil speaking, abuse) be banished from you with all malice (spite, ill will, or baseness of any kind" (Amplified Version)"**

> *"Get rid of all bitterness, rage, anger, harsh words and slander as well as all type of evil behaviours.  Instead, be kind to each other, tenderhearted,*

*forgiving one another, just as God*
*through Christ has forgiven you"*[57]
*(Life Application  New Living Translation)*

Polycarp, the convert of John the beloved at the age of eighty-two, started to embark on a trip to Rome, to confess before the Roman authorities that he was a love prisoner of Jesus Christ.  They tried to dissuade him from preaching Christ in every town through which he went, by letting him know that death by fire is the consequence of his love for Christ.  He was made up in his heart to preach Christ in Rome.
No sooner he arrived, than he was arrested and tried immediately, yet he refused to recant.

They tied him to the stake and set him ablaze.

The Roman authorities pleaded with him to blaspheme the name, Jesus Christ.
With pity he looked at them and said, "I have served this master nearly eighty years. I love Him. He is my Lord". With a firm voice he shouted, "light your fire" and in the midst of the flame he cried out, "Father, forgive them, they know not what they do".

Death by fire is a painful way to die.  But in the midst of this torturing flame, Polycarp forgave those that hurt and put him in the flame because of his belief in Christ.  There is no limit to forgiveness. You are expected to forgive all that hurt and mistreated you.

# THE FREQUENCY
# OF FORGIVENESS

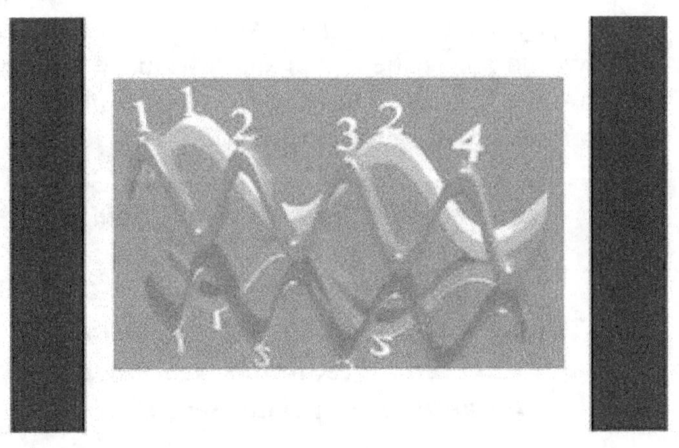

*"...Lord, how oft shall my brother sin against me,
and I forgive him? Till seven times?
Jesus saith unto him, I say not unto thee,
until seven times; but until seventy times seven".
Matt. 18:21-22*

There are people who keep bad records of evil done to them. They keep records of the names of those who offended and hurt them and how many times they were offended.

This made them to develop a resentful, negative, bitter, angry and vindictive attitude.

The above was a typical background of Apostle Peter. Apostle Peter believed that there was an extent one may offend or hurt you, and you retaliate. Peter was of the opinion that, if one forgave up to seven times, he was a righteous man. Then over and above seven times you can retaliate against anyone that offended you. He thought that Jesus would subscribe to his suggestion. Jesus gave him a shocker by increasing the frequency of forgiveness in geometric progression.

> *"Then came Peter to him, and said,*
> *Lord, how oft shall my brother sin*
> *against me, and I forgive him?*
> *Till seven times?  Jesus saith unto him,*
> *I say not unto thee, until seven times;*
> *But until seventy times seven"*[58]

What Jesus was trying to initiate here when he said, "forgive seventy times seven" which mathematically yields to 490 times, is not that we should keep bad records and start counting the number of times we were offended or hurt but that we should make forgiveness a habit.

He is telling us that under no condition should we keep any unforgiveness in our hearts, but should forgive those who offend us.

The message Jesus wanted to pass across to every one of us was that, **"we should continually forgive until it becomes a habit". So,** He wants us to get addicted to forgiveness.

I know you would want to say but Ken, "It is too hard to forgive and as a matter of fact, I don't think that I can forgive that man, woman, boy or girl for hurting me so deeply".

*"Ken, How possible is it for me to forgive, after he robbed me, molested my wife, killed my mother, and now claims to be a Pastor?  Should I forgive him and listen to him when he is preaching?"*

*"The man dis-virgined my little girl of about 6 years old and now you said I should forgive, how can I do that?"*

*"My husband slept with my younger sister; and now she is pregnant for him, and you still want me to forgive, how can that be possible?  I will never forgive him".*

*"My driver slept with my wife and they were caught red-handed, and now you said I should forgive?  How can that be possible?"*

Friend, I know it's too painful, but the bible says forgive; even Jesus while at the point of death, he still forgave them that nailed Him to the cross. Please, you just have to forgive and let it go off your heart.

You can forgive, for there are men who were hurt deeper than you were, yet they forgave.

Jesus forgave those that offended and hurt him.

Job forgave those that mistreated him.

Stephen amid pain of death forgave those that stoned him to death. David also forgave King Saul.

You too can forgive no matter the offence, because God commanded you to do so.

# CHAPTER TEN

# LOVE: THE CHANNEL OF FORGIVENESS

*"Love is the channel through which forgiveness flows from the offended to the offender".*
*Ken. K. Oparaku*

No relationships exist or flow smoothly without love. Love is a lubricant. It lubricates the wheel that holds every human relationship together.

**"Without love", according to
Apostle Paul, "we are just empty
noise makers"**[59]

*"love is the highest level of spirituality"*
Kenneth Copeland

You should understand that loving your neighbour as yourself is the secret of forgiveness.

Love should be the topmost priority in any relationship, and this love is unconditional and selfless. If love is lacking in your life, it means that you are a walking corpse. Apostle John said;

*"We know that we have passed from
death unto life, because we love the
brethren. He that loved not his
Brother abided in death"*[60]

This implies that Love is Life; you can only live it through the help of the Holy Spirit.

According to Peter Ustinov,
*"Love is an act of endless forgiveness".*

*Jesus admonished, "A new commandment
I give unto you, that ye love one another;
as I have loved you, that ye also love
one another, by this shall all men know*

***that ye are my disciples, if ye have
Love one to another'[61]***

From the above scriptural reference, I therefore define love, as "the true identity of Christians by which the world sees Christ through us".

***The bible says that,
"He who does not love does not
Know God, for God is love"[62]***

Love is the litmus test to show if you truly know God.

***"Yet Christianity without love
is just another cult" John Hagee***

Love, therefore, is the channel through which forgiveness flows from the offended to the offender.

You will find it most difficult to forgive that man, woman, girl, boss, neighbour, or friend that offended you, until you decide to walk in love. This is because our capacity to forgive one another depends much on our capacity to love one another.

That person you say you find it most difficult to forgive, I guess, is because you have not decided to show him or her love, an unconditional and selfless love.

When we love "inspite of" and not "because of", there is no offence or hurt that we cannot forgive.

Friend, God is calling you this day unto the life of love, so as to be able to forgive those who have offended you. There is no hurt or pain you cannot forgive; only if you can love.

**For he who can love, can also forgive.**
One thing you should understand is that, *"forgiveness will not be possible until genuine and unconditional love is born in your heart".*

Show me a man who finds it difficult to forgive and I will show you a man who finds it difficult to love.

Love and forgiveness are like Siamese twins that cannot be separated. Remember always that you are a debtor to everyone who offended or would offend you. Sometimes people do or say hurting and provoking things against you, in such a case, it is necessary that you give them love so that forgiveness will flow through it.

*The bible says,*
*"that we should owe no man*
*anything except love"*[63]

This is what makes all humans debtors.

"Love" is an action word. It is also a "giving" word. God expects us to give forgiveness to those who offend us through unconditional love.

*"One pardons to the degree that*
*one loves" Francios De la Rochefoucald*

The problems, sicknesses, calamities and woes

some people are passing through now, might not have come if they had given love and forgiveness to those who offended and hurt them..

*"To forgive is the highest, most beautiful
form of love.  In return, you will receive
untold peace and happiness,,
-Robert Muller*

*"Beloved, let us love one another; for
love is of God; and every one that loveth
is born of God, and knoweth God.
he that loveth not knoweth
not God; for God is love"[64]*

Jesus who is love personified brought a new kind of unconditional love called **"AGAPE"**
He demonstrated it in his day to day walk and dealing with men. And he expects us to love others unconditionally, thereby having the capacity to forgive those that hurt us everyday.

The primary ministry of the Holy Spirit is to build the divine nature of God, our heavenly Father into us. When this divine nature of God is built into us, we will begin to love even as God does.  If we are practitioners of love; there is no hurt, mistreatment, offence, blackmail, gossiping, frame-up, sexual assault, infidelity, heart  break and other emotional injuries that we cannot forgive.

The bible said that,
*"Love covers the multitude of sins"[65]*

Friends, let love have its perfect work in your life. You cannot have the capacity to forgive anybody if you fail to measure your relationship with other people with the yardstick of love. Love does not hate, it is not selfish, love is not bossy and it does not hold unto bitterness, malice, resentment, anger or hurt.  Love forgives and covers the multitude of offences.

To love is to have the nature of God and to have the nature of God is to forgive, and to forgive is to experience the wonders of forgiveness.

# CHAPTER ELEVEN

# THE WONDERS OF FORGIVENESS

*"To forgive means to give up or to let go all resentment, revenge and unforgiveness, so as to restore oneself to basic goodness and healthy relationship with others".*
*Ken. K. Oparaku*

It is amazing what forgiveness can do in the lives of those who practice it. I learnt that through forgiveness a cancer patient was totally healed, a stroke patient also received her healing because she released those that she locked up in the prison house of her heart. Also through forgiveness lost properties, wealth and relationship had been restored. To some other people, favour started flowing into their lives, families and businesses just because they realized the efficacy of forgiveness.

Forgiveness, indeed, had also restored the presence and the glory of God in some ministries.
In fact, time and space may not allow me to itemize all the wonders of forgiveness.
Do you know that some of the things you are passing through, are not caused by witches and wizards, evil men and women, but are caused by **UNFORGIVENESS?**

If you want to be happy and glad, if you want to be free, if you want to enjoy good health, if you want to enjoy long life, if you want favour, if you want abundant blessing, if you want promotion, if you want the presence and glory of God to go with you, if you want to succeed in your exams and other life endeavours, if you want to be fruitful in every area of your life, or you want everything that has been stolen from you to be restored, Just try as much as you can to get that unforgiveness, malice, resentment and bitterness out of your heart, and you will see the wonders of forgiveness. Job let go resentment and bitterness and prayed for his friends. Subsequently, he saw the wonders of forgiveness.

> *His health was restored,*
> *wealth, riches, properties and children*
> *were restored and his strained and*
> *severed relationship with others*
> *was fully restored.*[66]

Also, a wonderful sister, Holy Ghost-filled and tongue-talking, for good twenty-five years kept unforgiveness, resentment, malice and grudges against her biological brother and within this twenty-five years this woman was imprisoned by unforgiveness, she was diagnosed with cancer. But it happened that her church was having a programme and one of the guest speakers spoke on forgiveness very extensively, elaborately and in details.

Consequent upon this teaching on forgiveness the Holy Spirit dealt with her and convinced her of the need to forgive her brother, which she did promptly and from her heart she released him and let him go.

The next day of the same programme, she was going and as she was to enter into the church auditorium, she felt as if a million kilogrammes of weight was lifted off her and she felt very cool and light. Little did she know that, it was then that the spirit of cancer left her.

Till today, there has been no trace of cancer in her system. God healed her because she from her heart forgave her brother. She practically saw the wonders of forgiveness in her life.
The wonders of forgiveness was also visibly and practically experienced in the church of one of the

great preachers of the gospel known throughout the whole world.

## What really happened?

This great man of God was not in good talking terms with another great preacher of the gospel.

The two men of God kept resentment, bitterness and unforgiveness against each other to the extent that it affected their members also.

They were using placards against themselves with offensive words written on them. They hated themselves with passion. For conscience sake, their names are hereby withheld.
But the Almighty God, who would not like any one to perish but repent, started dealing with both of them.

A day came when one of these pastors was having a programme, the other pastor drove to that venue and quietly went into the hall and sat at the back seat.

He never knew that the host preacher saw him. No sooner had he sat down than he heard, "with Jesus joy shall we welcome to the rostrum our very big brother and a great preacher of the word, Evangelist AB. He stood up and went straight to the altar and they embraced themselves so warmly and firmly and tears began flowing down from their faces.

Immediately, the power of God came down most miraculously and the blind began to see, the lame began to walk, the dumb began to speak, unusual things started happening, diverse and numerous miracles took place. It was recorded that the miracles that took place that very day they forgave each other had not taken place ever since they started their ministries.

Friend, there are some miracles that will not take place until you forgive. The more you delay forgiving that person that hurt you, the longer your miracle is delayed.

According to Larry James,
*"To forgive means to give up, to let go", it also means to restore oneself to basic goodness and health. When we forgive, we are willing to give up resentment, revenge and obsession. We are willing to restore faith not only in ourselves, but also in life itself. The inability or unwillingness to do this causes harm in the one who is holding unto the anger."*

If you want to experience the wonders of forgiveness, you have to ask for the grace to forgive everyday of your life.

# GRACE FOR FORGIVENESS

*"No hurt is too hot enough to hurt a man whose heart has been anesthetized by 'GRACE'. Ken. K. Oparaku*

*"...For it is a good thing that the heart be established with grace" Heb. 13:9B*

The grace of God is very fresh and new in every single day of our lives. God knows very well that we are going to be faced with hurtful experiences that can make us not to feel like forgiving the one who offended us, therefore he provides for us everyday, the grace for forgiveness.

Forgiveness is not something we have to do, but something we must allow to flow through us by the power of his grace. When we stay within the circumference of the consciousness of our human nature and fail to allow the grace of God to flow through us, we will find it most difficult to forgive.

Therefore, what is 'grace'? Grace is the divine ability from God through the Holy Spirit to do what we couldn't have ordinarily done as human beings.

*"And he said unto me, my grace is sufficient for thee; for my strength is made perfect in weakness. Most gladly therefore will rather glory in my infirmities, that the power of Christ may rest upon me"[67]*

To forgive is not very easy, humanly speaking, but it is very possible because grace has made it so.

No matter how you pretend, one thing is sure and that is, 'it is not easy to forgive but it is possible by grace'. Because it is not easy to forgive, that is why we run to the Grace of the Almighty God, who supplies it to us.

*"Let us therefore come boldly unto the throne of grace, that we*

*may obtain mercy, and find grace*
*to help in time of needs"*[68]

The level or degree of offences are not the same. Some are lighter while some are heavier. At any level or degree of the offence or hurt, there is a corresponding grace to cushion it. Hence, the Holy Spirit through Apostle Peter encouraged us to grow in grace.

**"But grow in grace, and in the**
**knowledge of our Lord and**
**Saviour Jesus Christ.**
**To him be glory both now**
**and forever, Amen"** [69]

Grace heals the hurts, pains, wounds and unforgiveness. How does Grace do It? Grace does it like a surgeon, by anesthetizing the very particular area of the hurts, pains or wounds (the heart), so that the remembering of it is surrounded by the peace of God.

**"It is a good thing that the**
**heart be established with grace"**[70]

When God through his grace anesthetizes the heart, it becomes insensitive to insults, offences, embarrassment, gossip, back biting, blackmail and other hurts and there will be no offence, hurts or pains no matter how great they are, that you cannot forgive.

I see the Lord God Almighty anesthetizing your

heart with grace to forgive that your spouse who has been unfaithful to you; your uncle who killed your parents, your friend who betrayed you, that man or those young men who sexually assaulted you, your neighbour who mistreated you, your father or mother who abandoned you in your childhood, your brothers and sisters who took advantage of you, and that man or woman who blackmailed you.

The story of Joseph recorded in Genesis 45:1-10 gives us a classic example of how God can anesthetize one's heart to forgive his offenders.

The Lord God Almighty has made his grace available for us  to forgive those that offended and hurt us.

GRACE, GRACE, ABUNDANT GRACE TO YOU.

# CHAPTER THIRTEEN

# MAKE ME LIKE A CHILD AGAIN

*"When 'GRACE' captivates the heart,
it makes a man to forgive like a child".*
*Ken. K. Oparaku*

It is very alarming and disheartening what malice, bitterness and unforgiveness have done in homes, families, marriages, schools, organizations, work places and in churches. Brethren in the same department in the church are keeping malice, bitterness and unforgiveness against one another.

Unforgiveness has taken over the position of the Holy Spirit in the hearts of some Pastors.
Senior Pastors will not talk good about assistant Pastors and assistant Pastors will not talk good about the senior Pastors.
Blackmailing and witch hunting one another have become the order of the day in some churches. People on the same altar, lifting up their seemingly holy hands unto the Lord in worship and adoration, are not in good talking terms with one another.

The glory and presence of God have been suffocated by the lingering malice, bitterness and unforgiveness in the churches today, thereby making it impossible for the Holy Spirit to flow or demonstrate His power. The Holy Spirit cannot flow and demonstrate His power in the atmosphere of hatred, bitterness and unforgiveness, but in the atmosphere of love. Where there is love, there is unity, peace, understanding and the brethren will be doing things in one accord, and the Holy Spirit will find it easier to move.

> *"And when the day of Pentecost*
> *was fully come, they were all*
> *with one accord in one place.*
> *And suddenly there came a sound*

*from heaven as of a rushing
mighty wind, and it filled all
the house  where they were
sitting. And there appeared unto
them cloven tongues like as
of fire, and it sat upon each
of them. And they were all
filled with the Holy Ghost, and
began to speak with other tongues,
as the spirit gave them utterance"*[70].

When the Holy Ghost is allowed to have his way in our lives, He will captivate our hearts through the power of the word of God and He will make us to be like a child again.

Children don't keep malice, bitterness, unforgiveness and guile in their hearts.  Children are sincere, open, they forgive easily and they don't keep malice nor bitterness.

Something happened that was supposed to be a lesson to every man or woman that wants to learn. A couple with their child of about five (5) years of age went to visit a family friend of theirs. The host family also has a little boy of a similar age of the guest couple's child.  Both families were deep in their discussion and were carried away so much so that they never knew when the two kids started fighting to the extent of injuring themselves before they were separated.

Twenty minutes after they were separated, the child of the host family went into their kitchen and came out with a plate of rice with two spoons, he gave one spoon to the other boy and they sat down and started eating.  When they finished dealing with that plate of rice, both of them went outside and started playing.  Any one that saw them eating and playing would not believe that they were the ones that fought an hour earlier. Both parents started laughing when they saw them eating and playing together.

"This is how life is supposed to be" both parents said.  Hence the prayer, Lord, make me like a child again.
It is because of this that God in His word said,

> *"Brethren, be not children*
> *in understanding; howbeit*
> *in malice be ye children,*
> *but in understanding be men"*[72]

When the Holy Spirit anesthetizes our hearts with grace through the word of God, then do we begin to be insensitive to malice, bitterness and unforgiveness as children do.

Jesus emphasized much on the bitterness-free, malice-free hearts of the children and also how lowly and unassuming children are.

He made the following remark:
> *"And Jesus called a little child*
> *unto him, and set him in the*
> *Midst of them, and said,*
> *Verily, verily I say unto you,*
> *except ye be converted and*

> *become as little children,*
> *ye shall not enter into the*
> *Kingdom of heaven.*
> *Whosoever therefore shall*
> *Humble himself as this little*
> *child, the same is greatest*
> *in the kingdom of heaven"[73]*

I believe that, Charles F. Parham must have prayed that God should make him like a child again. And this was the reason why he was able to forgive Wilbur Volivo in all that he did to him. Parham, the father of Pentecost, gave himself to restore the revolutionary truths of healing and the baptism of the Holy Spirit in the body of Christ.

But Volivo, the General Overseer of Zion was using Waukegan Daily Sun, San Antonio Light and other publications to rubbish and scandalize the name of Parham. In 1907, a national news paper came with a headline that read, "an Evangelist, Charles F. Parham has been arrested", The story said Parham was charged with sodomy, a felony under Texas law. Volivo was bent on destroying the public image, integrity and reputation of Parham.

Though wounded by those he thought were his friends, he never backed away from the cities to which God had led him. Parham from his heart forgave Volivo.

Before he died on January 29, 1929, he made the following powerful statements:

*"I think the greatest sorrow of my life is the thought that my enemies, in seeking my destruction, have ruined and destroyed so many precious souls".*

*"I am living on the edge of the Glory Land these days and it's all so real on the other side of the curtain that I feel mightily tempted to cross over".*
*" I can't boast of any good works I have done when I meet my master face to face, but I can say, I have been  message He gave me, and lived a pure, clean life".*
*"I challenge you today to take account of your life, to count the cost, and to analyze where you stand in the area of faithfulness".*
*(See God's Generals, by Roberts Liardon)*

Also, Martin Luther King Jr. in one of his powerful sermons, told the story of how Edward Stanton humiliated, scandalized, ridiculed and castigated Abraham Lincoln when he was campaigning for president.
Stanton had declared himself the bitterest enemy of Abraham Lincoln.

*Stanton said, "If anybody must be president of United States, it must not be Abraham Lincoln."*
He considered Lincoln incapable, unqualified, ignorant, naive, ugly and tall, lanky man unfit for the post of the President. But inspite of all that Stanton did, Lincoln was able to win and became the 16th president of the United States. In nominating his cabinets, he did what shocked the whole world by nominating Edward M. Stanton as his secretary of war.

His relations, friends and advisers said, "Lincoln, are you so foolish, do you know what Stanton has been saying about you? Do you know the harm he has done to you? Did you read all those derogatory statements that he made about you?" He answered, "Oh yes, I know about it; I read about it; I have heard him myself. But after looking over the country, I find that he is the best man for the job".

# CHAPTER FOURTEEN

# LET THIS MIND BE IN YOU

*"Let this mind be in you which was also in Christ Jesus". Phil. 2:5*

At fall in the garden of Eden, man lost the glory of God in him, consequently his heart became polluted and corrupted, filled with bitterness, malice, unforgiveness, vindictiveness, selfishness, wickedness, deceitfulness and other evils.

> *"The heart is deceitful above all things,*
> *and desperately wicked who can know it?"[74]*

No human has an answer to this question, but God alone. The condition of a natural man's heart negates the nature of God, which He intends that man should possess.

God is never at any time comfortable with the depraved nature of man's heart. Hence, He initiated a supernatural Heart Dialysis and Transplanting (SHDT).

> *"A new heart also I will give you,*
> *and a new spirit will I put within you,*
> *and I will take away the stony heart*
> *out of your flesh and I will give*
> *you an heart of flesh"[75]*

God said, He will take away the stony heart out of your flesh and give you the heart of flesh.

The stony heart He is talking about is the heart of unforgiveness, bitterness, malice and wickedness.
It is also a stubborn, disobedient, rebellious and adamant heart.

*"Yea, they made their hearts as
an adamant stone, lest they should
hear the law, and the words which
the LORD of hosts hath sent in
his spirit by the former prophets;
therefore came a great wrath
from the LORD of hosts"* [76]

With this adamant stone kind of heart, humans find it difficult to forgive and forgiveness is the bed rock of Christianity. Remove forgiveness from Christianity, it becomes an empty religion like others. For you to be able to forgive those that hurt and offended you, God has to carry out a Supernatural Heart Surgery and Transplanting within you, by taking away the stony heart out of your body and putting in you the heart of flesh.

The heart of flesh is the heart that fears God and draws closer to know Him through His word.

*"And I will give them one heart,
and one way, that they may
fear me forever, for the good
of them, and of their
children after them"* [77]

*"And I will give them an heart
to know me, that I am the LORD;
and they shall be my people,
and I will be their God;
for they shall return unto
me with their whole heart"* [78]

The heart of flesh is what God wants us to have, if we must be like Him and forgive as He forgives, love as He loves, care as He cares, show mercy as He shows, give as he gives etc.

> *"Let this mind be in you,*
> *which was also in*
> *Christ Jesus"*[79]

No man can possess the mind of Christ without giving his heart to absolute study of the word of God with deep meditation upon the word.
You can't attain to this height by mere prophetic declaration and positive confession. There is no magic about that, it takes only disciplining yourself to search the scriptures persistently and consistently.

> *"But whoso looketh into the*
> *perfect law of liberty,*
> *and continueth therein,*
> *he being not a forgetful hearer,*
> *but a doer of the work,*
> *this man shall be blessed*
> *in his deed"*[80]

> *"But we all with open face*
> *beholding as in a glass the*
> *glory of the Lord, are changed*
> *into the same image from*
> *glory to glory even as*
> *by the spirit of the Lord"*[81]

As you give your heart to the study of the word of

God and to meditate upon it, so as to possess the mind, nature and characters of Christ, God is able to make all grace abound toward you, that you may always forgive from your heart, those who hurt, offended, maltreated, abused, blackmailed and critically dealt with you ruthlessly.

Pastor Chris Oyakhilome said "some people are quick to blow their top and become easily infuriated when others offend them, but when you are conscious of your identity as a Christian, you would learn to subdue your anger always. You would learn to love and appreciate others even when they hurt or mistreat you. That's the way of Christ; that's the life of a Christian.

May the Holy Spirit of God, through this book give you victory over UNFORGIVENESS, malice and bitterness and may He bestow upon you **THE SUPERNATURAL POWER** to forgive even as Christ forgives.

Remain rapturable always.

**MARANATHA**

**Kenneth Kelechi Oparaku**
**General Overseer**
Heaven Mindset Christian Centre (HMCC)
Lagos, Nigeria.
Phone No. +2348026401548; +2348064602180
E-mail: kennethoparaku@gmail.com

# BIBLE REFERENCE

1. John 16:33
2. Luke 17:1
3. Gen 3:1-19
4. Gen 3:21
5. Rev 13:8
6. Eph 1:4
7. Gen. 3: 8-10
8. Luke 17:1
9. Acts 24:16
10. John 3:16
11. Matt. 6:14-15
12. Heb. 10:17
13. Psm. 103:12
14. Prov. 4:13
15. Prov. 17:22
16. 1 Sam 24:5-17
17. Acts. 7: 59-60
18. Luke 6: 37
19. Job 42:10-11
20. Mark 9:23
21. Eph 4:31-32
22. 1Thess. 5. 14-16
23. Prov 17:22
24. Phil. 4:4;
25. Heb. 12: 15
26. 1 Sam. 25: 30-38
27. Mark 11:25
28. Matt. 18:34-35
29. Gen. 34:25-31
30. John 5:19
31. Gen. 49:5-6
32. 2Tim. 4:14
33. John 18:10
34. I John 3:2
35. II Peter 1:4
36. I John 4:4
37. Eph 2:4-6
38. Eph 1:21
39. Psm.51:3
40. I John 1:9
41. Rom. 6:11-13.
42. Matt 17:21

# BIBLE
# REFERENCE

43. John 5:39

44. Psm. 119:165

45. Job 42:10

46. Act. 7:59

47. I Cor. 13:11

48. John 13: 34-35

49. I Peter. 4:8

50. Rom. 3:29

51. Eph.4: 31-32

52. Matt. 6:14-15

53. Heb 12:14

54. I Thess. 5:13

55. Eph. 4:31-32

56. Matt. 18:21 - 22

57. 1 Cor. 13:1  10

58. 1 John 3:14

59. John 13:34  35

60. 1John 4:8

61. Rom. 13:8

62. I John 4:7-8

63. I Peter 4:8

64. Job 42:12-16

65. II Cor.12:9

66. Heb.4:16

67. II Peter 3:18

68. Heb. 13: 9B

69. Acts.:2:1-4

70. I Cor. 14:20

71. Matt 18:2-4

72. I Cor. 14:20

73. Ezek. 36:26

74. Zech. 7:12

75. Jer. 32:39

76. Jer. 24:7

77. Phil. 2:5

78. James 1:25

79. II Cor. 3:18

# PRAYERS

❖ Every gene of bitterness, malice and unforgiveness recycling in my family lineage or generation, be rooted out in the mighty name of Jesus Christ, Amen.

❖ Abba Father, by virtue of the authority bestowed upon me, I command every gene of anger and unforgiveness flowing in my blood to dry up and flush out in Jesus Name, Amen.

❖ My Heavenly Father, help me through the power of the Holy Spirit to do away with any root of bitterness, malice, and unforgiveness that can hinder my sweet communion with you. Also open my eyes to see things I need to do and things I need not to do to make my relationship with others a smooth and cordial one, that the world may see the resemblance of Christ in me, in Jesus name, Amen.

## PROPHETIC DECLARATION

❖ I confess, I am the righteousness of God in Christ Jesus. I am a joint heir with Christ. I am seated with Christ in the heavenly places, far above all powers.

❖ What is possible with Christ is also possible with me and what is not possible with Christ is not possible with me. It is not possible that Christ can keep bitterness and unforgiveness in his heart, therefore I cannot keep any bitterness, I have the life and nature of Christ in me, therefore I live a godly life, because I possess the DNA of Christ in me. I exhibit godly love and I have day by day forgiven any one that wrongs or offends me. Loving  and forgiving others naturally flow in me, in Jesus' Name, Amen.

❖    Abba Father, I thank you so much because I am your divine project and you are at work in me, in Jesus' Name, Amen.

❖    Abba Father, I thank you so much because I am your divine project and you are at work in me, making me to have grace to love and forgive those that wronged  or offended me.

❖    I Confess and declare that I will continue to love and forgive my offenders no matter the degree of the  offence(s) and promise never to keep any malice, anger, or unforgiveness in my heart against anybody anymore, anywhere and any time, in Jesus Name, Amen.

-

WE ARE PRAYING FOR YOU!!!

Join Kenneth Kelechi and Juliet Allagoa Oparaku and all Heaven Mindset Christian Centre (HMCC) family as we teach and learn how faith in God's Word can transform and build you up, make you to be conformed to the image of CHRIST and give you an inheritance  among all the Saints with the hope of seeing Him as He is when He shall appear in the air. HALLELUJAH!!!   Remain steadfast, faithful and rapturable till He comes and that's very soon MARANATHA!!!

**FOR PRAYER & COUNSELLING,**

CALL:     +2348026401548;+234064602180

WRITE:   Kennethoparaku@gmail.com